A WARNING TO CONQUERORS

by Donagh MacDonagh

HAPPY AS LARRY

DONAGH MAC DONAGH

A WARNING
TO
CONQUERORS

WITH A PREFACE BY NIALL SHERIDAN

DUFOUR EDITIONS

*Set in Janson type and printed at the Dolmen Press, Dublin
in the Republic of Ireland for
Dufour Editions Inc.,
Chester Springs, Pennsylvania* 19425

Library of Congress Catalog Card Number 68 - 26023

CONTENTS

[5]

Acknowledgement is made to the Clarendon Press and Mrs.
Mary Murphy for permission to translate five poems from
'Early Irish Lyrics' by Gerard Murphy and to *The Atlantic
Monthly*, *The London Magazine*, *Lilliput* and *The Irish
Times* in which some of these poems first appeared.

PREFACE

Thirty-four years have passed since Donagh MacDonagh and I made a joint literary début with a small volume entitled *Twenty Poems*. So it is, perhaps, sadly appropriate that I should have the melancholy task of writing a few words of introduction for this new volume of his work, which appears a few months after his untimely death.

Together with *Veterans* and *The Hungry Grass*, this latest (and, unfortunately, last) volume should help greatly to consolidate MacDonagh's reputation as a poet. Though he wrote with ease and grace in many forms — criticism, satire, ballads, verse drama — he thought of himself primarily as a poet and saw the world always with the clear eye and gay imagination of the poet.

A Warning to Conquerors strikingly underlines the breadth of his interests, the variety of his inspiration, and the technical skill and virtuosity which marked his finest work. Here we find once more his lyrical joy, his deep sense of history, his skill and grace as a translator, and the special vitality and gusto which he brought to the ballad forms in which he delighted to work.

Donagh MacDonagh was a brave and generous spirit, a gay companion and loyal friend. He bore with dignity a name which his father, Thomas MacDonagh, had already ennobled and he has left us a legacy of words which will keep his own memory alive and fresh for later generations. Out of a life which had its own share of sorrows his gay and gallant spirit forged works which have given joy to many thousands.

In his earlier volume, *Veterans*, he gave us his own proud testament:

> I offer to age and time
> A cold integrity,
> The moment's revelation,
> The clear intensity

Of the slender blade of thought
Keen through the finest chink,
Love dazzling in the memory
Between an eyelid's blink,

Joy that sings in the blood
The heart's extravagance,
I offer to age and time
To stay their swift advance.

It is an offering which age and time will not reject.

NIALL SHERIDAN

I

ON THE BRIDGE OF ATHLONE—A PROPHECY

I see them a mother and daughter
At dusk in a grass-grown lane
An old road from nowhere to nowhere
Where time has been slain
A mother and daughter ragged
And brown as a bird on a tree
Hair tangled and coarse as the bushes
Eye clear as the sea
And the land is a sea all about them
A green sea of grasses and trees
A pole like the mast of a wrecked ship
Trails its wires in the breeze
And the only things living are insects
And rabbits grown strong again
And the women haggard as madmen
From hunger and rain
And the daughter comes running and crying
—I saw on the Bridge of Athlone
A man, O mother a man there
And he's passed and is gone—
And men are so few now in Ireland
That mother and daughter cry
As one might mourn the last angel
A kingfisher gone by
And they weep for the land that is desolate
Green and empty that once was hard-won
Lot's daughters with no Lot and no wine-cup
To get them a son.

A WARNING TO CONQUERORS

This is the country of the Norman tower,
The graceless keep, the bleak and slitted eye
Where fear drove comfort out; straw on the floor
Was price of conquering security.

They came and won, and then for centuries
Stood to their arms; the face grew bleak and lengthened
In the night vigil, while their foes at ease
Sang of the stranger and the towers he strengthened.

Ragweed and thistle hold the Norman field
And cows the hall where Gaelic never rang
Melodiously to harp or spinning wheel.
Their songs are spent now with the voice that sang;

And lost their conquest. This soft land quietly
Engulfed them like the Saxon and the Dane—
But kept the jutted brow, the slitted eye;
Only the faces and the names remain.

SEÁN Ó DUÍR A' GHLEANNA

from the Irish

One morning rising early
The summer sun was shining
I heard the huntsman's warning
And sweet song of the birds,
The badgers ran before us
The long-billed wood-cocks calling
The echo hollow-sounding
And guns that loudly roared:
And there on rock was red fox
The huntsmen hal-holooing
And brooding in the pathway
A woman counts her geese—
But now the woods are falling
And we must fly to shelter;
Oh Seán O Duír a' Ghleanna
Your lordship soon will cease

That is my greatest sorrow
The shelter of my head down
The north wind knocks me over
And death is in the sky;
My merry dog is chained up
No exercise or frolic
Who used delight the children
In the brightness of the day
The only noble who is left now
The bounding stag, broad-antlered,
Who'd live his life on furze-tips
Through all eternity.
If I should have some quiet
From the Gentlefolk around here
I'd make my way to Galway
And leave this gaiety!

[13]

The plains, the streams the valleys
Are left bereft of leaders
And in the Street of Goblets
no health nor life is drunk;
And alas there is no shelter
From Cluain Stuaic na gColum
The hare is left to wander
By Ross's wandering bank
What are they at, the English,
This slashing and uprooting?
No more will thrush or blackbird
Melodiously sing;
And great now is the rumour
Of war when priests and people
Oppressed, despised ane herded
To barren mountain glen.

It is my grief this morning
I didn't die unsinning
Before I earned reproaches
From my own kith and kin;
But oh! the long, fine daytime
The trees with apples scented
And oaks with leaves replendent
And dew upon the grass
While I am wrecked and landless
Am lonely sad and friendless
Long lying in the hedgerows
Or in a mountain pass.
If there's no peace forthcoming
From the Gentlefolk around us
I shall desert this holding
And quit this world of sin.

STONEY BRENNAN

for Charles J. Haughey

He lived in Loughrea
When to steal was a capital crime
So he died in his prime
For the theft of a turnip that grew
In a privileged garden
He died without pardon
Was hanged and cut down
And laid out to grow cold on a stone
Which he soon made his own
For some simple sculptor unknown
To the arts as to memory
Hacked out an effigy
Rude and brutish:
Two circles for eyes, a triangle for nose
Mouth caught in the pose
Of a scandalized bishop
As sharp and as cold as a knife
Or an unloved wife.

And they set Stoney Brennan in stone
To watch over the town
With a goggle-eyed frown;
And there he is still
The confident god of the place
Whom women embrace
With a kiss on the Eve of New Year
Being certain that love
Will be theirs before Shrove—
Or a husband at least;
And the husband will kiss the stone face
When his head's in disgrace
For Stoney's remembered and loved
For his curative powers
And people bring flowers
And dance in the street to his memory,

Greater crowds than were there
When he danced on the air
For stealing a turnip
When that meant your head in a snare.

THE VILLAINOUS KERRYMAN

from the Irish
for Seósamh O hÉanaigh

I

THE GIRL If I follow after you straight back to Carbery
I'll be losing my mind if you don't come along
with me;
O Ro, I'll be crying down tears.

THE MAN Without lovely money don't you travel after me
With bank notes and sovereign coins from the
Englishry;
O Ro, to pay for the beer,
We'll have no blistered fists from digging in
misery
Or milking the cattle that give milk so grudgingly,
Oh never, but dancing with joy and with jollity,
Throwing out silver in sheer hospitality;
O Ro, the whiskey that cheers.

II

THE GIRL I'd walk over Wales and the world in your
company,
Not stay here in Ireland to hear Mass in piety;
O Ro, to New England we'd steer;
But two-thirds of your chatter is lying and
flattery
And the other one-third is seduction and roguery;
O Ro, it's your wildness I fear.

THE MAN O love of my breast you're the star of the day
to me;
I cannot be lying, whatever they say of me,
I'd fear for my soul if I dlandished with falsity,
You are caught in my breast and I'll die if you
banish me;
O Ro, I'll be stretched on a bier.

[17]

III

So I marched through the Callans and she came
    along with me,
Hearing my lies and the best of good poetry;
O Ro, the lying that cheers;
Till I emptied her pockets of every last moiety,
No beggarly cuteness, but true liberality;
O Ro, the journey was dear.
Then I settled my beaver and strode on most
    manfully,
My stick of shillelagh I carried unflaggingly,
Jumped hedges and ditches, while she ran
    remorselessly,
Spanked close to Kanturk with no maidenly
    modesty;
O Ro, she ran like a deer.

IV

When night-time came on and there was no
    sign of me
The gullible creature began to search frantically;
O Ro, the sound of her tears.
She burst out lamenting and wailed of dishonesty,
Roared, 'Money and heart are betrayed by some
    rapparee!'
O Ro, through many a year.

THE GIRL   Rise up friends and neighbours and help me
    search properly
In quest of this villainous rogue of a Kerryman
Through meadows and bogs to recover my
    property
For his blatherskite villainy left me in penury;
O Ro, my lesson was dear.

attributed to EOIN RUADH Ó SÚILEABHÁIN
[18]

PREAB 'SAN OL

from the Irish

The many methods of making money
Leave little leisure for having fun
And think how long you'll be stretched and breathless
Alone and lonely beneath a stone;
If you're a Lord or a Duke or Princeling
You'll take no gold when you go below
And therefore think that the greatest wisdom
Is making merry with Preab 'san Ol.*

The Gombeenman in his greed for money
Will take ten gains for the price of one
The cheapest goods will be priced the dearest
For what costs sixpence he'll charge a crown;
But as the camel can thread no needle
The Gombeenman if he'd save his soul
Must therefore think that the greatest wisdom
Is making merry with Preab 'san Ol.

The ship that sails on the pathless ocean
No chart no sextant to shoot the sun
Will yet in Spain or in Rock Gibraltar
Find friends to meet with when day is done;
The Grand Seignior in his airy palace
May see bags filling and call for more
And yet death waits so the greatest wisdom
Is making merry with Preab 'san Ol.

The lovely lily that toils nor spins not
Arrayed in beauty that's like the sun
But Solomon in his wit and wisdom
Could not stand up to comparison;
In life there's nothing but puff or bubble
An arrow loosed or another bowl
So therefore think that the greatest wisdom
Is making merry with Preab 'san Ol.

Lit. A Leap in the Drink.

THE BALLAD OF JANE SHORE

What her father's name was or where she was borne is not certainly knowne: but Shore, a young man of right goodly person, wealth and behaviour, a goldsmith, abandoned her bed after the king (Edward IV) had made her his concubine. Richard III causing her to do open penance commanded that no man should relieve her: which the tyrant did not so much for his hatred to sinne, but that by making his brother's life odious he might cover his horrible treasons the more cunningly.

MICHAEL DRAYTON 1637

As she went down through Lombard Street
To make her open penitence
Her cheeks that never blushed before
Were warm in her defence.

A linen skirt her only dress,
All London stopped and wondering,
A taper in the little hand
That once had held a king.

Bare to the waist, as though she rose
From the reluctant, amorous sea,
Raindrops were pearls that garlanded
Her hair's pale filigree.

Her body, white as waxen taper
Crowned at the head with golden light,
Had ripened in a shop of gold
To be a queen by night;

And she was young and womanly,
None saw her without love or pity,
Now stripped, who lived for gay apparel,
Now shamefaced, who was witty.

Proper she was and fair of body,
A grey eye merry, a slender figure,
An ankle that a man might span
Between a thumb and fiinger

And she had been the king's gay love
Who now must beg forsakenly
From those who would be beggars still
But for her charity;

But love that's light—once lovers die—
Is as a blade that courts the rust:
The evil deed men write in marble,
The comely one in dust.

IRISH POETS

Little they have to bind them but the name
Of Irishman and poet. Wilde and Swift
Ledwidge and Ferguson could but proclaim
That from one source there flowed a common gift
And Yeats when offered an extended sword—
Arise Sir William—chose to be the friend
Of Fenian John O'Leary at whose word
Only the sword of violence could descend
And Shem the Penman waiting for the voice
Of Shaun the Post to call him home to peace
Hated and loved the land that steeled a Joyce
To Argo out and seize the golden fleece.
They were all brothers like the Irishmen
Who take from their still hands the living pen.

LAMENT FOR PÁDRAIG DE BRÚN

They have said it all: 'The poet and the scholar,'
How he translated Aeschylus in his prime,
'The head like Everest,' 'The laughing blush,'
But what is there to rescue him from time?
A young man's mind, an old man's memory
Forgetting nothing that it once had known
Or read or heard or talked about all night,
All came to flower that scholarship had sown.

He walked with Raftery and Sophocles,
Catullus and Alighieri were his kin
And Owen Roe O'Sullivan, whose dying words
Were a regret he could no longer sin;
All these and recent men whose poems lived
In this man's mouth, this old man's memoried breath—
Old only in the years that grew on him
As ivy on the oak it chokes to death.

Who once had seen him never could forget;
He was the enemy of knave and bore,
Stupidity he loathed, but stupid death
Has him at last where wit can sing no more.

LÍADAN TELLS OF HER LOVE FOR CUIRITHIR

from Early Irish Lyrics *No.* 35

Unpleasing
The deed I did
What I loved I killed.

Were it not
For fear of Heaven
I'd have risked the Devil.

Not small
What he desired
To avoid fire.

A trifle
Vexed him towards me
I loved him greatly.

I am Líadan
Cuirithir I loved
Easily proved.

A little while
I was in his company
And it was sweet to me.

Forest music
Used to sing to me
And the fierce sea.

I had thought
Nothing I could do
Would change his view.

Conceal it not
He had my heart
Others my art.

A roar of fire
Has split this heart of mine
Without him I pine.

Now the way she vexed him was her haste in taking the veil.

THE LAMENT OF CRÉIDE FOR DÍNTERACH
from Early Irish Lyrics *No.* 36

The arrows that murder sleep
At every hour in the cold of the night
Are love-lamenting for the night-hours
Spent in company and delight.

Great love for a man of another land
Who excelled all others has taken my bloom
Little my colour, slow my step
I have no sleep now in any room.

Sweeter than all songs was his speech
Save holy adoration of Heaven's King,
A glorious flame without a boastful word
A slender mate to whom a girl might cling.

When I was a young girl I was modest
Lust for man was no concern of mine,
Since I have come to the uncertainty of age
My wantonness has begun to glow and shine.

I am tormented by it, O chaste Christ,
His grievous death who was wounded in my sight,
These are the arrows that murder sleep
At every hour in the cold of the night.

ON THE LOSS OF A PET GOOSE

from Early Irish Lyrics *No.* 37

O Mór of Moyne in Mag Síuil
No bird deserves such grief as this,
You too must die, so why lament
A goose that only knows to hiss?

Daughter of stalwart Donnchad think
Of all the stories you should know,
Have you forgotten in your haste
That more than geese have gone below?

Conn of the Hundred Battles went,
Surely you've heard, and Cormac too,
And Art, his son, and his grandson—
They could fight death no more than you.

The wrathful and the gentle lie
In the same earth, Cú Chulainn's breath
Is stopped, but not by mortal man,
Not even he could outrun death,

And that great warrior, royal Finn,
Fergus, whose name tipped every wave,
And Mannanán; O Mór, recall,
These with your goose are in the grave.

In Brían's Ireland there are geese
At your command, lament no goose,
Brían rules Munster, take your choice,
The king, though great, is generous.

GRÁINNE'S SLEEP-SONG FOR DÍARMAIT

from Early Irish Lyrics *No.* 55

Sleep a little, just a little
There's nothing to fear
O lad to whom I've given love,
Sleep Díarmait my dear.

Sleep soundly, oh so soundly
Díarmait my love
I shall watch over you
Hovering above.

Sleep a little and bless you
Above the water's edge
Above the lake-top foam
Close to the sedge.

May your sleep be like that
Of every true lover
Who carried off his love
All Ireland over.

I shall watch over you
O my Grecian battle-fence
My heart would almost break
Without your presence.

To part us one from the other
Is to break a family
Taking children from parents
Or soul from the body.

Sleep a little, just a little
There's nothing to fear
O lad to whom I've given love
Sleep Díarmait my dear.

THE FAREWELL OF OISÍN SON OF FINN
from Early Irish Lyrics *No.* 57

These hands have been withered
These deeds are undone
These powers are prevented
The ebb-tide has come.

Great joy and great profit
Thank God once were mine
Long is the day now
I was fair in my prime.

Once I was beautiful
Light women I enjoyed
Not weakly I leave the world
My springtide's destroyed.

For this failed fasting wretch
A morsel on a stone
A morsel on this withered hand
A morsel on a bone.

HURLING FINAL

It is not only crowds as thick as sand
Nor crowd-delighting field of Irish green
Nor the familiar off-key strutting band
Spellbound forever at the age fourteen!
No, nor the coloured hats, rosettes and flags
Mingled and hostile, nor the cries and cheers
Futile advice and joy like paper bags
Puffed out and banged and bursting in our ears;

The hour is all these things yet more than these;
It is delight in movement as exact
As music, or Euclidean syntheses
Where theory once accepted becomes fact;
It is the beauty of the perfect act
When moving bodies can become abstract.

THE GARDENS

In no rich robes of Babylonian stuff
The Maiden walks the simple garden dreaming
Of quiet marriage to her carpenter;
From her still beauty tree flower and gilded bee
Borrow new loveliness and the courtly fountain
Mirrors her grace; tuned to her steps the music
Of all nature is grown sweet until
From the magnificent heaven falls a shining
Messenger dazzling the earth, announcing
Tidings more terrible than ever brazen
Trumpet sounded in peace or war. The Maiden
Bows in obedience to that awful word
And in the garden spring light is blasted and
The air is rank with smoky torches dim
With presage of a Saviour betrayed.

JUST AN OLD SWEET SONG

The pale, drooping girl and the swaggering soldier
The row-dow-dow-dow of the stuttering drum,
The bugles, the charges, the swords are romantic
For those who survive when the bugles are dumb.

The lice of the trenches, the mortars, machine-guns,
The prisoners exchanged and the Christmas Day lull,
The no-man's-land raid and the swagger-stick rally
Are stirring, for when was a finished war dull?

The road-block, the ambush, the scrap on the mountain,
The slouch-hat, the trench-coat, the raid in the night,
The hand-grenade hefted, police-barracks burning
Ah, that was the life, and who's hurt in a fight?

The blitzkreig, the landings, the victories, the losses,
The eyes blind with sand, the retreat, the alert,
Commando and D-Day, H-Hour and Block-buster
Have filed through the glass, and was anyone hurt?

A flash and a mushroom, a hole in the planet,
Strange growth in the flora, less fauna to feed
Peace enters, the silence returns and the waters
Advance on the earth as the war tides recede.

II

SONGS FROM PLAYS

LOVE DUET

I am a poor girl and my heart it is breaking,
Betrayed by a young man so handsome and bold,
For he's left me to follow a rich merchant's daughter
Because I am poor and she's decked out with gold.

HE

I am a poor lad with a heart full of sorrow,
In love this twelve months with a maiden so fair,
But she's given her heart to a treacherous young man
And passes me by with her head in the air.

SHE

My heart broke in two when that young man betrayed me,
One half is still his, but the other is mine;
If I gave half that heart is there any would take it
And hope that the two might unite at some time?

HE

Oh, who is so rich as to spurn half a sovereign?
So hot in his leather to scorn half a sun?
The half moon is fragile and sweet when she's shining,
And the half of a diamond is better than none.

With a heart and a half I will take up your offer—
By simple addition that makes our hearts two.

BOTH

Forget all the past, we've the present and future
To find what you get when you add true and true.

FROM NOW TO EASTER SUNDAY

If all the tinkers now in town
Could pool their wealth and smelt it down
In whiskey every man would drown
From now till Easter Sunday.

Chorus

Laughing, cheering, dancing, drinking
Breaking windows, cursing, winking,
Always happy never thinking
From now till Easter Sunday.

If every tinker that you meet
On road, on bohereen or in street
Could choose if he would drink or eat
He'd drink till Easter Sunday.

If all the cans that he had sold
Were overflowing with bright gold
He'd buy no miserly leasehold
He'd drink till Easter Sunday.

Had he the wealth that Damer had
He'd spend it like a decent lad
In making other tinkers glad
From this till Easter Sunday.

So, if a tinker you should meet
Don't pass by looking at your feet
Invite him in and stand a treat
He'll stand on Easter Monday.

SONG OF THE TINKERS

I have been a tinker all my life,
I'll die a tinker laddie O,
Unwashed, uncombed and carefree as
My hundred year old daddy O.
And just like him I'll have ten wives,
Or twenty if they're willing O,
I'll dance and sing and have my fling
As long as I've a shilling O.

Chorus

Then, high-ho, the tinkers O,
The willing, swilling drinkers O,
Beneath the sky what men can vie
With Ireland's clinking tinkers O?

Oh, the merchant locks his wealth away,
In safe, in bank, or stocking O,
The tinker spends it while he may
Nor finds such conduct shocking O.
The lawyer, doctor, priest invest
Their cash in stocks so risky O
The tinker wiser than the rest
Invests it all in whiskey O!

Oh, the men who wear a collar white
As fresh milk or the driven snow
Must work, bend over, while it's light
For what small pay they're given O
But the tinker, loving, cursing, free
Would find such service penal O,
He may be poor, but such as he
Need nurse no duodenal O.

Chorus

Then, heigh-ho, the tinkers O
The willing swilling tinkers O
Beneath the sky what men can vie
With Ireland's clinking tinkers O?

[37]

BARLEY AND GRAPE

The grape and the barley are grown for our pleasure,
They swell in the generous sun,
They're pressed and distilled to rejoice us and gladden,
They freshen the old and the young;
They warm the cold-hearted and cheer the down-hearted,
Raise love-thoughts in girl and in boy,
They rally the faint-hearted, quicken the great-hearted;
Barley and grape are our joy.

Chorus
Then clink glasses, drain glasses,
Fill glasses, drink glasses,
Let's leave no gay song unsung:
While we've bottles and throttles
Let's put in our noddles
The stuff that makes old fellows young.

The sun on the cornfield, the sun on the vineyard
Are bottled against the cold days,
The frost cannot harm us as long as we arm us
With summer sun's medical rays;
An apple a day keeps the doctor away,
A bottle a day keeps him well,
So for medical reasons we swallow the seasons
When Grape and John Barleycorn swell.

Chorus
Then clink glasses, drain glasses,
Fill glasses, drink glasses,
Let's leave no gay song unsung;
While we've bottles and trottles
We'll put in our noddles
The stuff that makes old fellows young.

THE TOUCH OF MIDAS

The old philosophers sought for a stone
For turning lead to gold;
But we do better, we take poor men
And make them rich and happy and then
We take a girl ice-cold,
We dance her round the fire and then
We kiss her, and then we kiss her again
And we warm the girl that is cold.

Old Midas had a magical finger
Which turned all things to gold;
But we do better, we take rich men
And make them poverty-stricken and then
We take a girl that's bold,
We dance her round the fire and then
We kiss her, and then we kiss her again,
And we love her for being bold.

BORROWING

Oh, a girl that loves a tinker lad
Must learn the tinker ways,
Must eat when hungry, drink when dry
And thrive on giveaways;
She must know the tinker way of life
And borrow all she can—
We borrow all that's not nailed down
To feed the tinker clan.

Oh, a girl that loves a tinker lad
Must share her father's purse
With those in need, remembering
That property's a curse;
She must spot the hiding place of wealth
When she sells a pail or pan,
We borrow all that's not nailed down
To feed the tinker clan.

Oh, a girl that loves a tinker lad
Is happy all her days,
She needs no silk or satin blouse,
No camisole or stays
She has treasure, pleasure, plenty as
She borrows for her man,
We borrow all that's not nailed down
To feed the tinker clan.

DRINKING SONG

Good fellows, let us drink to-night
As no man drank since Bacchus;
The sky will be our cocktail jug,
The lakes and seas our glasses

Chorus
And when the sun comes up again
And sees the mighty slaughter
He'll say, 'The earth is rolling drunk,
They should have stuck to porter'.

The merchant and the exciseman
And all who live in houses
Will be our footstools, and the hills
Our seats through carousels

We'll pour the brandy, gin and rum,
The whiskey and the sherry
Down gullets thirstier than sand
And all die drunk and merry

Then burn the corks and pour the liquor,
Empty all the bottles,
You'll get no drink once life is past
So pour it down your throttles.

THE INVITATION

Will you come to the bower through the bog and the
    heather,
To the fires where the boys and girls are met together,
Where the dancing board is laid down, where accordion
    and fiddle
Are gayer than the poteen with their merry tarra-diddle,
Will you come, will you, will you,
Will you come to the bower?

You can drink tea or porter and eat scallions while you've
    able
Your seat is the bogland and the heather is your table,
The moon for a lamp and the little stars above you,
And a young man at your elbow to encourage kiss and love
    you,
Will you come, will you, will you,
Will you come to the bower?

You can dance jigs or reels or a half-set or the lancers
And you'll shine in the midst of the fairest of the dancers;
Will you sing like a blackbird on the highest branch of
    morning
Or whisper words of love when the holy day is dawning?
Will you come, will you, will you,
Will you come to the bower?

Will you come to the bower, since the sun, that old reprover
Has gone to his bed, left the world to lass and lover,
Since the stars wait to deck you and the moon comes out
    to greet you,
Will you come from your room, life and love are here to
    meet you?
Will you come, will you, will you,
Will you come to the bower?

THE HOT WEATHER BALLAD

Oh, the sugar and the tea-twist and the bread,
The chicken and the duckling for the pot,
The potatoes and the carrots and the onions from the garden,
Oh, who wouldn't be a tinker when it's hot.

The night-shirt from the clothes-line or the hedge,
The blanket from the cupboard or the cot,
The pony from the stable and the bottle from the table,
Oh, who wouldn't be a tinker when it's hot.

The daughter or the mother from the man,
The truncheon from the Bobby when you're caught,
The bacon from the chimney and the porter from the
    sheebeen,
Oh, who wouldn't be a tinker when it's hot.

The woodbine in the hedgerows and the lanes,
The Fair Green and the organ's gay gavotte,
The love-making in the haystacks when the stars are bright
    as tapers,
Oh, who wouldn't be a tinker when it's hot.

THE BALLAD OF SAINT JOHN

Saint John was a man with a mission,
He lived in a very poor way,
He ate locusts I'm told for his breakfast
And drank water neat for his tea.

He was preaching hell-fire and damnation
And company-keeping he banned,
No Dance Licence ever was granted
While Saint John was abroad on the land

For dancing, he thought was unholy,
A shocking occasion of sin,
He advised the young men of the country
To avoid anything feminine.

Now there was a young one called Salome,
A divil to dance and to sing
And she took a great liking to Saint John
And she went to her father, the king,

'If I dance, will you give me a present?'
Says she, and the old lad agrees,
So she started to dance like an angel
And the king sitting back at his ease.

'Very nice,' says your man, when she's winded,
'Very nice, and now what will you have?'
'Oh, daddy,' says she, 'give me Saint John,
That lovely young man for my slave.'

'Fair enough,' says the king, 'you can have him.'
But Saint John, being a saint, said 'No fear.'
So Salome was mad, and her father
Said, 'Right, you can cut off his ear.'

'No, No,' says Salome, 'his head please!'
So she danced with the head round the Court,
And bonfires on John's Eve remind us
That dancing is dangerous sport.

SONG FOR A SINGER

If I could dance as I can sing
I'd ask no severed head
But living lips and living eyes
To teach me all love's pleasing lies
And play on my heart string
If I should please a king.

I'd not demand, if I could dance,
A man without a head,
But one who'd rise and dance with me
Through all love's choreography
And sweep me to romance
If I could sing and dance.

Were I King Herod's wilful girl
Who should have been abed
Instead of dancing in a veil,
I'd not demand a head from jail
As payment for my whirl
Were I King Herod's girl.

No, I would ask a finer
A braver better boon,
A gay young man to dance with,
A brilliant dancing moon,
A birdlight foot for dancing
Through all the miles of space,
Tunes from the constellations,
A starry dancing place.

So, if I chanced to please a king
I'd ask no young man's head,
But living ears and living eyes
To open on love's enterprise,
A mouth to kiss and sing
And play on my heart string.

THREE 18th CENTURY SONGS TO THE SAME TUNE

I: LOVE

Sweet is the music and sweeter the dancer,
Love is the question and love is the answer,
Soft now the light and the eyes and the singing
The night is half spent but our joy is beginning.
Soon in the shadows two shades will be straying
Soon in the darkness soft tunes will be playing,
Soon the white moon will come peering and prying
Soon, far too soon, our delight will be dying;
  Flying and dying and lost in the dawning,
  A memory, a dream, a romance before morning;
  The love and the laughter, the wine and the singing
  Will be lavender-lapped then—but now they're
  beginning.

II: DRINK

Fill up your glasses with punch while you're able,
There's good company under and over the table,
Drink hearty, drink largely, drink deep and drink often
There are few blows so hard that a drink cannot soften.
Punch is the nectar of poets and thinkers
Love is a will o' the wisp to good drinkers
So leave its beguiling and stick to the bottle
'Tis the good of the bottle that gladdens your throttle;
  Brightly and sprightly it livens your wit up,
  Soon every room in the mansion is lit up,
  Merrily, cheerily, airily ringing
  Hear the gay voices of good fellows singing.

III: DUELLING

In loving or drinking a word may be spoken
Too harsh or too sober—and by the same token
A silence is sometimes a subject for fighting,
A laugh or a frown may be equally slighting.
So stand to your pistol and blaze when you're ready,
Let your powder be dry and your finger be steady;
The dawn light is traitrous, its thin wind is cruel
So wrap yourself well when you're fighting a duel.
       Pistol to pistol or sword blade to sword blade
       The challenge is cancelled, the insult is unmade;
       Once blood is extracted the bill can be reckoned
       So drink or make love now—and I'll be your second.

THE LOVE SICK GIRL

Now sorrow has my heart
Captured in every part.
Now let my lips forget
Love's alphabet.
Memory forget his face
Arms his embrace.
Beat heart more coldly,
Stir blood more slowly,
Eyes learn to weep
And to keep
Secret and stern.
Now all my senses learn
New touch, new sight, new sound upon the ear,
New taste—and a new scent, the scent of fear.

All clocks will run slow
Or else cease to go,
The night be haunted by
Memory.
From dawn, when chanticleer
Rouses the torpid ear
Until the night will be
A century.
Farewell to happiness,
Gentleness,
The smile reflected by
A smiling eye.
Now winter has my heart, and bitterness
Freezes the foolish bloom of faithfulness.

Now I must walk
In nunnery and talk
Purely
And demurely,
Learn saints' names,
Light candle-flames;
And I must repent
Merriment,
Banish laughter
Hanker after
Martyrdom,
Kingdom Come,
Forget the coloured world and its brave sights,
Live but for heaven and its pale delights.

THE CLASSICIST

When Venus from the billows rose
She must have looked like you,
But lacked a modish gown to wear
Had only seaweed in her hair,
But you undressed or she in clothes
Would make a perfect pair.

Were all those golden girls in flower
Whose names are handed down,
Europa of the snow white bull
And poor Danae who found life dull
Until that famous golden shower
To you I'd give the crown.

Alas that Venus in the skies
Is far too seldom seen
But were she here and you beside
I'd not chose Venus for my bride
No, it is you who'd fill my eyes
And not a riggish queen.

For you share memories with me,
Your speech is not antique
It is not nectar that you drink
Nor of ambrosia that you think
The dress you wear is maidenly
While hers is all too Greek.

Should Botticelli's queen arise,
From Liffey's placid tide
With naiads working on her hair
And cupids floating in the air
I'd send her back to paradise
And keep you by my side.

A POACHING SONG

When God created water He must have thought of fish
And said, 'Let there be salmon to lie on Adam's dish!'
So he created Adam, for salmon must be caught
And flies too he created, and then of rods He thought;
So trees grew straight and slender, and Adam learned to fish
And thanked the Lord each evening for the brightness on
    his dish.

But who created bailiffs in a dark hour of the night?
Not God, Who loves good fellows and taught fish how to
    bite;
Not God Who has created the peaceful flowing stream.
The salmon ripe for taking when he leaps for joy in Spring.

A wise man, Fionn Mac Cumhaill, caught a salmon for his
    tea
That lived on nuts of knowledge, dropped from a knowing
    tree;
He cooked it and he tasted and knew all men could wish
And wise men ever since then sit by a stream and fish;
But men unwise and evil, prompted by vicious greed,
Forbid good men their pleasure in doing this good deed.

Let others praise the herring, the tunny, trout or whale,
Give me the noble salmon with lightning in his tail;
To monarchs leave the sturgeon, the carp of golden hue—
I'll snare the silver salmon, and share the dish with you.

GEORGIANS ON MY MIND

Here's to gold it makes you free,
Here's to yellow guineas,
Here's to cash and the Marshalsea
Where the gamesters play with pennies
For only fools consent to work;
Hurrah for all brave schemers.

Here's to the coin that's double faced,
Here's to the dice that's loaded,
Here's to the rogue that's thorough-paced,
And here's to the wretch that's goaded,
For only fools consent to work;
Hurrah for all brave schemers.

Here's to the decent, honest cheat
Who after money hankers;
Here's to the doxy on the street
And here's to the bank and bankers,
For only fools consent to work;
Hurrah for all brave schemers.

Here's to the card that cheats the eye,
Here's to the trick-of-the-loopman,
Here's to the gulls and what they buy—
God bless the nincompoopman,
For only fools consent to work;
Hurrah for all brave schemers.

THE SONG OF THE MARSHALSEA DEBTORS

FIRST DEBTOR

Behold the pauper's prison, the hell of bankrupt debtors
Where sadly we're repenting for our spendthrift, happy days,
Remembering the bottles that emptied down our gullets
The wigs, the lace, the satins and the ruinous displays
Oh, once I lived contentedly and friends I loved surrounded
    me
Care nor grief ne'er troubled me nor made my heart feel
    sore,
But now those days are over and here I rot in misery
Reflecting on the abstinence that fifty times I swore.

SECOND DEBTOR

'Twas dice that proved my downfall, the cards and little
    horses
Whose speed was far inferior to every other horse,
The fly I had my cash on alighted last invariably
My raindrop on the windowpane dried up, nor stayed the
    course;
But were I rich and young again and could I all I've lost
    regain
I'd live the same life out again, and luck would turn my
    way;
With dice and cards and claret the night would vanish
    rapidly
And I would rise triumphant at the closing of the play.

THIRD DEBTOR

A dark eye or a grey eye, an eye that's soft and tender,
A form that's tall and slender, a breast that stands at bay,
An ankle trim and shapely, a hand that's slim and playful
A mouth that's shaped for kissing and breath that's a
    bouquet—

[53]

These are the charms that ruined me, yet I pursued them
    foolishly
Certain that each new schooling would give me my degree;
But all a lifetime brought me the first girl could have taught
    me,
For all I ever learned of them was what they thought of me.

III

BALLADE WHICH VILLON MADE AT THE REQUEST OF HIS MOTHER TO PRAY TO OUR LADY

for Louis Roche

Lady of Heaven, queen terrestrial
Empress you are of the infernal heath
Receive me now, your humble prodigal,
Who would be one of those about your seat;
Not easily elected the elite.
Your many gifts my mistress and my queen
Are even greater than my sins have been
Without such gifts no soul could qualify
To enter Heaven—here no lie I mean;
        And in this faith I wish to live and die.

Oh, to your Son make this memorial
That He may all my sins, as I entreat,
Pardon, as He made beatifical
Saint Mary, at whose prayer even the effete
Theophilus, who in his great conceit
Had sold his soul, was through that go-between
Pardoned and cleansed, who was the most obscene.
Grant no such sin be shared by such as I,
Nor to the sacraments to go unclean:
        And in this faith I wish to live and die.

I am a poor old woman, one who shall
Never learn now to read or write a sheet,
But in my parish church where paradisical
Paintings are on the wall I see complete
Heaven with harps and lutes, and hell beneath
Where damned souls are tortured; on that scene
I look with fear, the other is serene.
So, confident and joyful, I apply
To you for succour, my lady and my queen;
        And in this faith I wish to live and die.

V irgin, you bore our Saviour, Who has been
I n being forever and Who never shall,
L ong as infinity is, conclude His reign;
L ady, He left His Heaven and took all
O ur weakness on to help us to the sky.
N ow I pray to your Son, the Nazarene;
       And in this faith I wish to live and die.

THE BARE DEAL BOARD

from the Irish

I would marry you without a cow, a pound or a counted
    dowry,
And I'd wed you against the wishes of those who would
    have us unwed,
And isn't it a dark disease that you and I are not in Cashel
    town
For we would be happy there, love, with only a bare deal
    board for bed.

Rise up, my love, and come with me to the glenside,
We'll have a bed of rushes, and air as light as our kisses,
Our music will be water murmuring under the branches
And the blackbird's song will wake us, and the song of the
    little linnet.

Pulse of my wrist, pulse of my secret heart
A poor thing it is that we are not joined by the clergy
The way that I'd know you were mine, and not need to be
    hating
Every man in the county whose eye might light on your
    beauty.

DEIRDRE

I: *The druid Cathbad, when the wife of Feidhlimid was brought to bed, spoke an obscure and puzzling prophecy.*

From the womb there cries
A woman with iris eyes
With foxglove cheeks
Pearls are her teeth
For her will there be many slaughtered
Among the chariot fighters of the North.

There screams from the womb's cave
One tall fair long-haired grave
For whom champions will contend
Whom High Kings will demand
Her teeth are ambushed by
Lips like the berry
And queens will be jealous of her
Matchless faultless to be remembered forever

II: HER BEAUTY

If one inch more were added or one half inch subtracted
She would be less than perfect.
One grain of powder more and she would lose that moon-bloom,
One extra touch of rouge would daub that perfect rose-cheek.
Kingfishers are her eyebrows, her teeth are little shells,
Her nails the wings of grasshoppers, her waist a roll of silk.
Her breasts are huntresses.
Her legs are straight, like saplings, silver in the bark
And curling in the foilage. Her hair, spilled moonlight.
Her lips temptation to the berry-picking birds.
Her voice the middle notes of a reed pipe
Melodious as a stream on summer nights.
And she is ripe as an apple
Shaped to the curving hand that plucks it down.

[60]

THREE SONGS BY DEIRDRE

I

What fair young man will win my heart,
What eyes admire my face?
What heart will quicken to my heart,
What face live in my face?
The skin as white as the snow that's drifted
The cheek that's as red as my blood,
The hair as black as the raven's wing—
So shall I know my love.

II

Were I a moony girl, unwed
Then I could pray for a hasty lover
To climb the wall and take me suddenly
Out where the waves are hoarse with passion.

Were I a pale, unwanted love-child
Then I could pray for a golden carriage
Abounding presents and a perfumed mother
Warm like a queen in a nest of fur;

But all I have is a heart that is pressed
Between rocks as heavy as druid altars
And a sigh that would swell a sail to Ireland.
What's there for me but the sea and its roaring?

III

Delightful to me the land of Scotland,
Dun Sweeney and Glen Etive, the Woods of Cuan
Where in the bending branches the cuckoo shouted;
Delightful in this land the flesh of salmon,
Not evil the flesh of venison, the strong flesh of badger;
Delightful are its lakes cupped in its mountains,
Where even the rain is bright, and the royal heather
Fit for a High King's coat. Here I was happy
Till love was quenched and all the colours faded.

[61]

A BALLADE OF POETS

Poets who in an earlier age
Might sing high deeds of chivalry
And win a Prince's patronage
To live in bardic luxury
To-day would find unerringly
A chair among the unemployed;
Their grandeur and their misery
Have been explained by Doctor Freud.

Poor Keats who had a haemorrhage,
Thompson who lived in penury,
Swift of the unrelenting rage
Is each a neat case history.
Chatterton's brilliant forgery,
Why Byron's taste for women cloyed,
Kit Marlowe's death through harlotry
Have been explained by Doctor Freud.

The robin-redbreast in a cage
Which caused Blake such anxiety
With Lesbia's sparrow on a page
Explains erotic imagery;
And Homer of the *wine-dark sea*
Had complexes we'd all avoid,
His sense and sensuality
Have been explained by Doctor Freud.

ENVOI
Sir, you have printed poetry
By paranoic and schizoid;
May modesty or pruriency
Be not explained by Doctor Freud.

THE JACKEEN'S LAMENT FOR THE BLASKETS

from the Irish of Brendan Behan

The sea will be under the sun like an empty mirror,
No boat under sail, no sign of a living sinner
And nothing reflected but one golden eagle, the last,
On the edge of the world beyond the lonely Blaskets.

The sun will be setting, the shadows of night dispersing
As the rising moon shines down through the sea-cold night
    cloud,
Her long, bare fingers stretched down to the empty earth
And the houses fallen and ruined and broken apart.

The only sounds the hush of the birds' soft feathers
Skimming over the water, returning safe and together,
And the wind as it sighs and softly swings the half-door
Mourning a hearth that is cold for ever more.

Oh, every feature of this horrid creature
Was distilled to torture the mind of man;
I whinnied from her, but life's a teacher,
And I took my course from this harridan.

So I stood Byronic and stage sardonic
In the Gothic ruins of Strawberry Hill,
With a well posed pose that was half ironic
I unslung my fiddle and trilled a trill.

As I played my bravest the night was tonguing
With a smothered sigh and melodic groan,
And out of the darkness appeared a young one
Sweet in the flesh and trim in the bone.

She was neat and sweet beyond all believing,
Her kiss was lighter than the butterfly,
Her eyes would brighten the dusk of evening,
And my fiddle sang at her softest sigh.

I've been long stravaiging the world and plaguing
The handsome girls with my slouthering mouth,
But that night of love has my heart reneging
The girls of the world from this day out.

I left her side as the day was dawning
And wandered down through the dreaming town;
There, through a window, I saw my darling
With corpse-lights burning at foot and crown.

It was no light sleep that my love was keeping
But death, and a week had those candles burned,
Her mother thought that my fiddle speaking
Might call her spirit from underground;

She had come as a ghost to that mouldering grandeur—
I left her there and my feet were slow;
I never again let my eyes philander.
I broke the fiddle and snapped the bow.

[65]

TWO SONGS OF CHILDHOOD

I: REFUSAL

To be one with this village, never aspiring,
Eyes turned in to its narrow street,
Living among its ruined fragments,
Learning soon to distrust and cheat,

Reared in ignorance, never innocent,
Knowing too much and too little too soon,
Fearing knowledge, praising cunning,
All music set to a ballad tune,

To be one with these people, to grow beside them
Like branches bent by a constant gale,
To be buried successful, since the nameless thousands
Having never ventured can never fail.

II: HYMN OF JOY

FIRST CHILD

Adrift on a sea of flowers
The white bog-cotton our waves,

SECOND CHILD

The powder-puff clouds for sails,
The bee for a gale.

FIRST CHILD

Our sailors are barefoot boys
And girls who dance on a deck
All coloured with dandelions
As recklessly gold as the clock
Keeping time in the sky.

SECOND CHILD

O and this is our stained-glass day,
With fuchsia and poppy as red
As Christ's heart, and the little daisies
The same that were meek to His tread.

FIRST CHILD

And the goldenrod is sweet
As the wild-rose,
And the woodbine makes incense
Where it grows.

SECOND CHILD

And the sun is a monstrance too
That blesses the fly,
The bee and the rabbit and hare
With its haloed eye,
And the finch in its chasuble
Of wings and of song,
And blesses the ox and the ass,
And blesses us all.

[67]

LOVE IN A HERB GARDEN

Under September's temperate, westering sun
The garden slumbers and is overrun
Where when the sun was bright as Goldenrod
We found that love's the only garden god.

I was the Scarlet Runner who ran down
Your Columbine, no Sage was I but clown,
A Common Fennel, wild in a Wild Thyme
Who Comfrey found to Salsify his prime.

You were my Lovage, sweet as Coriander
You were my Applemint and my Pomander;
Your Maidenhair unshorn, your aspect calm
And to my Catmint stare your eyes were Balm.

Alas, a Black Horehound was on our track
Wormwood and Baneberry launched their attack
My love lay bleeding then and turned to Rue
And where the Basil shone the Mugwort grew;

The Celandine deflowered and shrivelled up,
Elder and Bitter Bane were in my cup,
Angelica whose colours had been fine
Turned nicotine, as did my Columbine.

And yet when spring with customary rain
Wakens the herbs I know we'll love again
And in the middle of the brick-lined town
The god of gardens turn us upside down.

OLD POET ON A BEACH

Miserable for the shade that evening brings
He mopes upon the gold Canteras shore,
Laced-boots and careless hat and woolen scarf,
High-buttoned, warm against the winter-roar

Of angry winds in the bleak noon of March
In freezing Longford, two thousand miles away,
Where sun like this in a deranged mid-season
Might, once in four, unhinge a summer day.

Pale blue old eyes, wisest in all save guile,
That have outlasted all contemporaries—
The far-famed, selfish ones who sacrificed
Friend, kin and patron for the histories,

Sacrificed them in bitter spitefulness
For art's achievement, fame, on which men dote
As though it mattered, for fame follows there
As surely as the wake behind the boat.

Who furiously seeks for fame in his own time
Is as the aging harlot on the streets,
The future reads the end and only scholars
Curiously examine the discarded sheets

And coldly judge the variorum words
Of living works that glow or laugh or sing
By those who starved or sacrificed or died
So that their work might be a living thing.

He on Canteras beach alone survives
Into our age, in hope on the sea-wall.
Unhaunted by those ghosts his mind is still
Unjealous as the sun that shines on all.

Las Palmas, Nice, Dublin 1963 - 1966